DENNIS BYRD

DENNIS BYRD

by Dennis Byrd
with Michael D'Orso

ZondervanPublishingHouse
Grand Rapids, Michigan

A Division of HarperCollinsPublishers

Dennis Byrd
Copyright © 1995 by Dennis Byrd and Michael D'Orso

Requests for information should be addressed to:

ZondervanPublishingHouse
Grand Rapids, Michigan 49530

Library of Congress Cataloging-in-Publication Data

Byrd, Dennis.
    Dennis Byrd / Dennis Byrd with Michael D'Orso.
       p. cm. — (Today's heroes)
    Condensed from author's Rise and walk by Mark Littleton.
    Summary: The author discusses his faith and his football career and
how the two came together when he broke his neck while playing for
the New York Giants.
    ISBN 0-310-41251-X (softcover)
    1. Byrd, Dennis—Juvenile literature. 2. Football players—United
States—Biography—Juvenile literature. 3. Football players—Reli-
gious life—United States—Biography—Juvenile literature. [1. Byrd,
Dennis. 2. football players. 3. Christian life.] I. D'Orso, Michael. II.
Littleton, Mark R., 1950– . III. Byrd, Dennis. Rise and walk. IV.
Title. V. Series.
GV939.B97A3 1995
796.332'092—dc20
[B]   95-24268
                                          CIP
                                          AC

Printed in the United States of America

---

95 96 97 98 99 00 01 02 /❖ DH / 10 9 8 7 6 5 4 3 2 1

Contents

Chronology of Events

October 5, 1966. Dennis Byrd is born in Oklahoma City, Oklahoma.

Summer 1980. Dennis accepts Christ at a church camp.

Fall 1983. Dennis "comes out of nowhere" to star for the varsity football team his senior year at Mustang High School.

1984–89. Dennis plays for the University of Tulsa Golden Hurricanes.

December 20, 1986. Dennis marries Angela Hales.

Spring 1989. Dennis is drafted in the second round by the New York Jets.

July 11, 1990. Ashtin Byrd is born.

November 29, 1992. Dennis breaks his neck in a game against the Kansas City Chiefs when he runs into teammate Scott Mersereau.

December 9, 1992. Dennis begins rehab at Mount Sinai.

February 1993. Dennis goes home to Owasso, Oklahoma.

July 9, 1993. Haley Byrd is born.

1

The Hit

I remember lying there and looking up at the sky, a gray New Jersey sky, with a few thin clouds breaking it up. It was November, and the Giants Stadium lights were glowing above me as the buzzing inside my body began to subside. My first thought was, "Man, that was a good lick." I mean, hits like that don't happen on every play, and I was wondering what happened to the other guy. I had no idea the other guy had been Scott Mersereau, my own teammate.

I tried to get up, to push myself off the turf as I had a thousand times before, to turn toward the sideline for the coaches' hand signals to set our defense for the next play, to get on with the game. But as my head raised off the ground, I felt something give way. I heard it, too, a grinding and crunching at the top of my spine. And I knew right then. I had broken my neck.

No one else knew. Not yet. It was Mers the guys were worried about at first. He'd taken the hit in his sternum, his body violently recoiling from the blow, then going limp. He was down a long time, fighting to breathe as some of my teammates went over to help.

I slowly settled my head back to the ground. Then I raised my right arm to unsnap my helmet. But instead of going where I willed it, my hand thumped onto my face mask with a sickening clank. The sound of it, that hand hitting my helmet, is a sound I'll hear the rest of my life. It reminded me of the sound of the rain and hail that would pound the ventilation pipe of my granny's storm cellar back in Oklahoma as we all huddled in the glow of lantern light, waiting out the violence passing overhead. I'll never forget the sound in that cellar, that haunting, hollow sound. And I'll never forget the sound of my hand hitting that face mask.

Thoughts were beginning to tumble through my head. And one thought kept repeating itself: "Don't move. Don't move anything."

Kyle Clifton, our middle linebacker, was the first to come over. "Let's go, buddy," he said, expecting me to just jump to my feet. "Get up. Let's go."

"Kyle," I said, "I can't. I'm paralyzed." His face

turned pale, almost blank. Then Marvin kneeled by my side. Marvin Washington was my roommate and closest friend. "Dennis," he said softly, "what's the matter?"

"I don't have any feeling in my legs, Marvin," I said. "I can't feel my legs."

He lowered his voice, almost to a whisper. "Just try, baby," he hissed. "Try." He turned away. He had to. He didn't want me to see the pain he felt, the tears he was already wiping from his eyes. Marvin knew. They all knew by then. All my teammates and the Chiefs, too.

By now Pepper Burruss, our assistant trainer, was beside me. Pepper was always goofing, always pranking, always one of the guys, laughing and joking around in the locker room. But now he was somebody I'd never seen before, dead serious, totally in control. "Peppy," I said, "I can't move my legs. I broke my neck."

"Okay," he said. His voice had taken on a tone I'd never heard before, one I'd never had to hear. Utterly calm, utterly professional. "Just be still here," he said. "I got you. I'm gonna stabilize your neck."

Then he began reciting the things he was going to do to keep me from hurting myself more. He locked his hands on the sides of my helmet, holding my head in place. That's the way it would stay for the next nine hours, someone else's hands locked on my head, as if they had become a part of my body.

Within seconds Bob was there, too. Bob Reese, our head trainer, rushed over as quickly as he could.

And Steve Nicholas and Elliott Hershman, two of our team's doctors.

They were by my shoulder, with Pepper at my head as Bob asked me how I felt, what I could feel. I told him, "Bob, my neck's broken. I'm scared. Am I going to be paralyzed?"

He asked me what had happened. I told him I didn't know. I'd run into someone, but I didn't know who. I'd hit someone, but I didn't know how.

I could hear feet shuffling around up in the stands. An eerie hush had settled over the stadium. No loud noises. No shouting. I could feel them all looking at me.

My teammates were crowding in now, trying to see how I was, trying to say something. But now Bob was barking orders, unbelievably organized, calling for a back board and telling someone to get the cart out here. And while he was whacking off these orders, Jim Nicholas was asking me question after question. "How do you feel? What do you feel? Can you feel this?" And he'd move my foot or tap it. My toes, knees, groin area, stomach, hands, arms, chest—he worked his way along my body, pushing it and poking it with a pin, seeing what I could feel. And I *could* feel.

I could tell I was being touched but not the way you normally feel something touching you. It was a dull sensation. There was no acuteness to it, just a feeling of pressure.

"Can you move your legs? Can you move your

arms?" The answer to both of those was no. I had been lying there seven minutes on the Chiefs' eighteen-yard line when they finally rolled me on my side, slid the yellow back board under me, cinched me down with ties, strapped down my helmet, and lifted me on to the cart, with Pepper still holding my head. Steve Nicholas and Dr. Hershman climbed on and we took off. Joe Patten was driving as we headed toward the west end of the stadium, bumping over the turf, the whir of that little electric motor humming in my ears.

I took another look at the sky, not knowing it was the last look I'd get for a long time. And I began thinking beyond the moment. All sorts of thoughts. I wondered again if this would be the last time I wore this uniform on this field. I wondered when I'd get the feeling back in my legs. I wondered where Angela my wife was, how she was. And our little girl, Ashtin. She'd waited up for me the week before when we lost to the Patriots and I didn't get home till nearly midnight. Would she be waiting up tonight?

It seemed like there were a hundred people there as we turned into the tunnel, rounded the corner, and pulled up to the ambulance. Lots of commotion, lots of noise, and a sea of faces, including Jeff Lageman, one of my closest friends on the team, who was out for the year with a knee injury. He'd been watching the game from the press box.

"How do you feel?" Jeff asked, walking beside the

cart. "I can't move anything," I told him. Jeff looked stunned. Then he started talking, as if the scariest thing right now was silence.

"You'll be all right," he said. "You'll be all right. It's not gonna last. You'll be all right." Then Angela appeared. She was wearing her fur coat, the coyote fur I'd gotten her for her birthday, and she was crying hard, really sobbing. I knew how worried she must have been, watching me from up in her seat, seeing my legs totally still, not knowing how to get down to me, not knowing if she was allowed to be with me.

They loaded me into the ambulance, then somebody shut the doors. Suddenly everything was silent.

That was another sound I'll never forget. It was the sound of permanence.

2

The Byrd Brothers

The way my parents tell it, I almost died several times before I turned two. From the time I was six months old till the time I was two, I was in and out of the hospital with pneumonia. Every time my parents took me in, my mother wasn't sure if I'd be coming home.

The worst trip was the last, when they found a spot on my lung. The doctors sent me home that afternoon, telling my mother to bring me back in the morning.

That night I was extremely ill. I wouldn't eat. I could hardly hold my head up. My mother was holding and rubbing me, praying intensely, when my dad got home. She told him what the doctors had said, and my brother Doug overheard them.

Doug was only four years old, but he walked over, kissed me on the forehead, and said, "Jesus will make him better."

I was up and myself again in fifteen minutes. The lingering pneumonia, the spot on my lung—those things just disappeared.

At the time we lived in suburban Oklahoma City. Christianity was a big part of our home life. We'd go to church morning and evening on Sundays and on Wednesdays as well.

Evenings at home, my parents would sit on the bed. We kids crowded around them while my dad read a Bible passage or an inspirational story. He'd always read stories about someone who made it through a struggle. We'd talk about it, then listen to him read from the Bible. I loved those times.

But I was no angel when I was a boy. Once I flooded the attic after a buddy and I punched a hole through the roof tile so we could put up a homemade periscope and spy on the neighbors. Later that day a rainstorm hit, and my dad noticed water leaking from a ceiling light fixture. When he climbed up and pulled back the attic opening, he got soaked. And I got spanked.

Then there was the baby skunk I caught after my

dad showed us where the mother was raising her babies. He warned us to keep our distance, but I couldn't keep away. And I paid the price. I wound up stripped and naked in the kitchen, my mom scrubbing the skin off me. I got an entire bottle of my dad's cologne poured over me, and no one came close to me for a week.

When I was a boy, I trailed after my older brothers, Doug and Dan. We played Little League baseball, but the game we really loved was football. My parents didn't want us to play in any actual leagues, with helmets and pads, until we were older. They thought it was too rough. But no league could have been rougher than those games I played with my brothers out in the yard, tossing the ball and creaming whoever caught it. Neighborhood kids always came to our house to hang out, but when we pulled out the football, they took off. We were just too rough for them.

I had two younger sisters, too—Jeni and Dawn. I was closer in age to them than I was to my brothers, so when we played, it was usually my way. They'd be the Indians, and I was the cowboy.

When I was nine years old, we moved to California near my Grandpa and Grandma Byrd. My dad started a puppet show ministry, and every weekend the family would pile into our station wagon to drive to a church or school for a show. Afterward, we'd pull out the football and start clobbering each other out on the church lawn.

But it wasn't the puppet shows or the football that I remember most about that year in Elk Grove, California. It was something far more important and personal. It was my conversion.

3

A Gift of the Spirit

My conversion happened the summer before I turned fourteen. I was at a youth church camp in the mountains, the kind of place I went every summer, with plenty of outdoor activities and plenty of prayer.

Prayer has always meant a lot to me. My way of worship is very quiet, and it's certainly not limited to church. I pray all the time—driving to work, sitting out on a coyote stand, getting up in the morning. I thank the Lord for the things he's given me, for the things he's given all of us. I don't have to get down on my knees to pray. I don't even have to shut my eyes. I have always felt as though I can converse with God anywhere, and I do. But until that summer I had not felt the Lord speaking back to me.

I had heard grown-ups around me in church speaking in tongues. I remember being about six or seven when I first heard a woman talking in a language I couldn't understand, and I wondered why she was doing this. My mom and dad explained it to me, and I realized how emotional prayer and receiving the Holy Spirit can be. I saw it plenty of times after that, and it never disturbed me.

It was normal. In fact, seeing someone being moved like that was pleasant. But I had never been moved that way.

I had no reason to expect anything extraordinary to happen when we gathered one evening that summer at the church in the center of camp. It was a giant log cabin, and there were about seventy-five of us, mostly teenagers. We came together every night to worship as a group.

At the end of the evening there was an altar call, an invitation to come down to the front and pray. I'd gone down and prayed plenty of times, but this time something felt different. Something had shifted inside me. I'd always felt connected to God when I prayed, but I had never truly taken the Lord into my heart and fully given myself to him. Maybe I'd been too young. But now was the time for commitment. I could feel it, deep inside. I just knew now was the time to give myself to Christ.

I had been fortunate that my parents had raised me in a Christian home, but I understood now that I could not make it to heaven on their coattails. I had to make this decision on my own. I was accountable for my own salvation.

No voice came to me. No vision. This was a choice. It's something you just decide from the bottom of your soul. You have to want that gift to receive it. It's a very spiritual thing, something you really feel. That night for the first time I felt it. There were other kids around me feeling it, too. Pretty much everyone had come down. Some of them were crying and praising the Lord.

A lot of emotion swept through the room, lots of sobbing and tears of joy. I wasn't doing any of that, but I was praying in a way I never had before. I just continued praying softly to myself, and at some point I realized I was praying in a different language. It was happening to me! I was speaking in tongues! I was swept with incredible joy.

When I came home at the end of that week, I knew I had grown up somehow. I was growing up not just in years, but in terms of my relationship with Christ—and with myself.

4

The Pole

Near the end of my freshman year of high school, we packed up the RV and moved back to Mustang, Oklahoma.

Mustang is a small, quiet town. Most of the 10,000 people who lived there when we arrived were connected in one way or another with cattle ranching or farming, mostly wheat and corn. It was the kind of place where the center of social life, for the kids at least, was the Dairy Queen or the Sonic, complete with car hops. There was no traffic light in town, just a four-way stop at the intersection of Mustang Road and Oklahoma Highway 152, which ran through the center of town.

We stayed with my grandmother Price through that spring, my brothers and I living in the RV while my parents and sisters stayed with Granny in her trailer. To me it was a lark, like camping out.

We hadn't been there a week before Charlie Carpenter, Mustang High's head football coach, got a call from one of the school's counselors, a man named Terry Spencer. "Hey, coach," he said, "I've got these three new kids that just moved in from California, and two of them, you can't believe how huge they are. The third one, well, I don't think he'll make it."

I was about six feet tall, maybe 145 pounds. Not exactly a striking physical specimen. Dan was 6'3", 220 and Doug was 6'2", about 205. Big Byrd and Middle Byrd, they called them. I was Little Byrd.

The first time I ever wore a football helmet was that spring. That was all we wore—no pads, no hitting. Just light drills. I had good hands; I was pretty fast, so they put me down at flanker and outside linebacker. That's where I'd be when they really began playing football at preseason practice in August.

We were playing in the 3-A division, the state's next-to-largest classification. Choctaw, Chickasha, El Reno, Ada, Guthrie, Broken Bow, Tahlequah, Noble, Stillwater . . . these were the schools we played. And Yukon. The Yukon Millers. One town away, they were our arch rivals.

Mustang had a terrific program going. They

qualified for the state play-offs just about every season, and they'd been to the state finals the year before. Coach Carpenter had established quite a tradition, and my brothers stepped right into it. Dan was a senior, a tight end, and a good one. He split time with another guy, and Doug played varsity too, mostly on goal-line stands.

I was on the J. V. squad, playing on Monday nights in front of crowds not quite like the ones my brothers saw. But that didn't matter to me. I was hooked on this game. Sitting the bench for most of that fall didn't matter either. I knew sooner or later I'd get my chance, and finally, almost at the end of the season, I did.

We were playing Choctaw, we were way ahead, and they sent me in to help mop up. I remember the grass had turned from green to brown. It no longer had the supple feel of summer. Now it crunched underfoot. That's how late in the season it was. But I still felt the magic while I was running out there under those lights.

The first play was a running play to the other side of the field. I pursued, the guy cut back, and I tackled him. I'm not sure who hit whom. All I know is my mouthpiece came flying out and snot bubbles blew out of my nose. That's what happens if you get hit really hard and unexpectedly. All the air is pushed out of your lungs in a sharp burst and snot comes flying out with it. Anyone who's ever made or taken a hit like that knows what I'm talking about.

I'd never felt anything like it before, that impact, that strong, jarring sensation, that momentary bit of limbo as you're floating through the air before you hit the ground. I remember the guys picking me up and slapping me on the back. That was the first hit of my life, the first real tackle in a real football game.

And it felt fantastic. From that moment on, football totally consumed my life. I ate, drank, and slept this game. I loved the combat, that one-on-one, man-to-man competition, clean and direct. I was responsible for beating the guy facing me. Pure and simple. It was me against him. No maybes, no gray areas. Either he whups me or I whup him.

That's how I wound up with the pole. It was the end of my junior year. I had heard a story somewhere about a football player who built up his body by going one-on-one against a billy goat. Day after day he bashed and butted this goat, literally locking horns with the animal to toughen himself up. We didn't have any goats, but the dirt yard outside our family's trailer was nice and flat, a perfect place to put a pole in the ground.

I found a four-by-four green oak pole, about six feet long, sunk it about three feet deep, and began a routine that became my evening ritual that entire summer. By day I lived in the school's weight room, where Coach Carpenter had just put in a new set of free weights. Then, each night, as the sun was setting

and the air was cooling off, I'd go out to that pole and settle into a good, solid three-point stance. Then I'd fire out and slam that wood with my hands or my forearms, using the form and techniques my coaches had taught me. Over and over I hit that pole, until the sweat poured off me. I'd hit it until my hands actually bled. Then I'd hit it some more. I'd keep going until tears streamed out of my eyes.

That's when I knew it was time to stop, when the pain and exhaustion turned into tears. Only then would I finally drop to the dirt and call it a day. The next night I'd be back to do it all over again.

I had a dream by then. I told my parents and friends I was going to go to college on a football scholarship. Privately, I believed I was going to play professional football, too, although I had nothing to base that belief on but bare faith and determination. I shared that dream with no one. My friends gave me a hard enough time just for talking about playing college ball. I had a buddy, Rich Stukie, who'd crack up every time I mentioned it.

"Look at you," he'd say. "You haven't even played varsity ball yet, and you're talking about college? Man, you're crazy."

Well, I played varsity ball that next season. I definitely played varsity ball.

5

Varsity Year

They say I came out of nowhere my senior season at Mustang, and in a way that was true. I had played hardly any varsity football at all. I had never started a game. There had been no newspaper stories written about me, no headlines, no films or scouting reports filed in coaches' offices at other schools. Other schools didn't even know I existed. So when I started making waves that fall of 1983, people were stunned, even people in Mustang. They were asking themselves, "Is this the same kid?"

But I wasn't surprised. I knew I had put in more time than anybody else. If somebody was going to beat me, he was going to have to have worked harder than I had, and I didn't think that was possible. I knew how much I could give, how deep I could reach. I'd answered all those questions myself that summer.

I was 6'4" now, 205, and it didn't take long for other teams to begin noticing me. Pretty soon I no longer had just one man to beat. It was always two, then three. I remember having to beat first the tight end, and then the tackle. Then there'd be a running back in there, too, and I'd have to go through them all.

It was a great year. Noble, Guthrie, Western Heights, El Reno, Yukon—we mowed through the early part of our season with an average of more than 3,000 fans packing our stadium for the home games.

We were 5–0 before we lost our first game, to Carl Albert. Our only other regular season loss that year was to Chickasha in the tenth game. They beat us 28–14.

We finished 8–2 that regular season, good enough to get into the state play-offs, where we faced a school from Tulsa called Bishop Kelley in the first round. If any one game marked my high school career, that was the one.

Bishop Kelley had won the state championship the year before, and we weren't supposed to have a chance. Early in the first quarter they ran an option to my side, their strength against ours. The quarterback kept it, and I nailed him—along with the fullback, all in one blow. They had to help the quarterback to the sideline; he was done for the night. The very next play, they ran the option again, to my side again, with the new quarterback keeping it again. And I took out the whole backfield again, putting that quarterback out of the game. Charlie Carpenter told me he'd never seen anything like it in his life. They had to go with their third-stringer the rest of the way, and we won 30–6.

When the game was done, Tom Stockton, the Bishop Kelley coach, came over to Coach Carpenter and said, "Who is Number 68?" Coach Carpenter told him, and the next morning Stockton drove over to the University of Tulsa football department, where his good friend John Cooper was the head coach. Cooper wasn't in, so Stockton left a note on his door. "GO TO MUSTANG," it read. "RECRUIT DENNIS BYRD."

That year, after a lot of wrangling and going back and forth between colleges and recruiters, I decided to head to Tulsa and become a Golden Hurricane.

6

The Tulsa Hurricanes

At the end of my senior year in high school, I began to date Angela Hales.

Until then, I had never had a steady girlfriend. I was too interested in football to date much. But I began to notice Angela at church. She was a year younger than I was. I'd watched her sing many times in the church youth choir and with the school's musical groups. She was a tall blonde, the most beautiful girl I'd ever seen. One Sunday I turned to my mother and said, "Someday, Mom, I'm going to marry her."

I didn't have much money, so often Angela and I spent our dates watching TV at her house or going out to dinner with her parents. The fact that I was a big football star meant nothing to Angela. She wasn't even interested in the sport and never went to games until she began dating me.

Before I headed off to college, I bought Angela a "promise" ring. That fall during football season she and her family came up every weekend to see me play.

My first game as a collegian was at home against Texas Tech. I was scared going out to run defensive plays. But by the fifth game of that season, I'd done so well that Coach Cooper gave me my first start.

It was on my birthday, October 5, and we were playing against Oklahoma State. Their star at that time was Thurman Thomas, "Squirmin' Thurman." Thurman was already a superstar, of course. He had always been a superstar. I might have come out of nowhere, but everyone knew when Thurman was coming. The first play of that afternoon I actually nailed him for a two-yard loss. But I didn't see a lot of him the rest of that day, except from behind. I've still got a nice newspaper photo from that game of my chasing after Thurman as he shot up the sideline on his way to a 54-yard first quarter touchdown run. Thurman finished with 157 yards that afternoon— not bad, considering he only played the first half.

We wound up 6–5 that year, and I finished with the same number of tackles as my jersey number— forty-eight. I'd put on fifteen pounds and established myself as a starter at outside linebacker, which made it a little surprising when Mike Daly, our defensive coordinator, took me aside that spring and told me they were going to move me to defensive end. Still, I relished the change. I enjoyed playing linebacker, dropping off to cover the flat, but there was nothing I'd rather do than rush the passer, and that's what defensive end was all about.

When my sophomore season began, I was in my element, bigger and stronger than ever (I was up to 245 pounds), smarter after a season of experience, and playing in the place that would become my home for the rest of my career—the defensive line. I also had a reputation as a guy with a pretty reckless style of play.

We had a good season my sophomore year, the best in fact of all my years as a Hurricane. We went 7–4, including a win that is still considered probably the biggest in Tulsa football history.

It came in our third game of the year, against those Cowpokes of OSU. The largest crowd ever to see a game in Skelly Stadium arrived that Saturday night wondering how badly Thurman and company would run us over.

The first play of the game went just as the year before, with me nailing Thurman for a loss. We were already fired up, and that hit just stoked the flames. Years later Thurman still mentions some of the licks he took that game. When it was done, we'd held him to 88 yards, one of the lowest totals of his college career, and we had a 27–23 win they still talk about in Tulsa.

By the end of that year, I was really coming into my own. We played Wichita State, and in one series I sacked their quarterback, Brian McDonald, twice for twenty-five yards in losses, then knocked him out of the game as he let go of a pass on third down.

Two weeks later we played top-ranked Miami at the Orange Bowl. We lost 23–10, but I sacked Vinny Testaverde twice and fell on a fumble to set up a field goal. We thought we had a shot at bowl game that year, but it didn't happen, which was just as well, because Angela and I had made plans to marry. We said our vows on December 20, 1986, at the Mustang Assembly of God Church. After our honeymoon, we returned to Tulsa, where Angela went to work in an insurance office, and I went back to school ... and football.

The next two seasons for the Hurricanes weren't great. I wondered if I would even be noticed by the pros. But I played well, exceptionally well. And I got noticed by the scouts. When the pro draft came around, I was a contender. All in all, many teams contacted me—Minnesota, Green Bay, the Cowboys. Eventually the New York Jets got very serious.

Draft day Angela and I joined a crowd of friends and family at my parents' house in Mustang. Like dozens of seniors around the country, I had a crowd around me, watching TV, waiting for the selections to start.

I was extremely nervous. What if things didn't go the way the Jets said they would? What if I wound up someplace else? The Rams had told me they might try to get me at the end of the first round. The Vikings tried to trade up to beat out the Jets early in the second. I didn't know what was going to happen. When the Jets' first pick came up—the 14th pick overall—and they took Jeff Lageman, I figured, okay, so far so good. Neither the Rams nor the Vikings made a move. The first round ended, and it went into the second. Finally it was the Jets' turn, their pick for the second round, the 42nd overall selection of the 1989 NFL draft . . . Dennis Byrd.

That was it. I was a New York Jet. The house went nuts. My dad and brothers rushed to a nearby sporting goods store and bought every Jets cap they had—three.

Later I made a special trip back to my family's old place, just to remind myself where I'd come from. It was a classic April afternoon, clear and bright. And quiet. The place was deserted.

Angela was with me, and she sat in the car, tears in her eyes, while I got out and walked over to the pole. Weeds were grown up around it now; it was weathered and gray, but it was still there.

I had always told myself that if I ever made it, if I

ever got to the point where I was leaving Oklahoma behind, leaving my roots, I'd take some of those roots with me, something I could always touch to remind me of where I'd come from.

I had brought a can with me. Nothing fancy, just an old coffee can. I bent down and filled it with dirt, the same dirt I'd sweated and bled into back when I wasn't sure what I'd become, when all I had was a vague dream.

Now that dream had come true. I was going to play professional football. I was going to live in New York City, farther from Mustang than mere miles could measure.

And I was bringing some of that Oklahoma soil with me.

7

Rookie Year

It wasn't a month after the draft that I flew into minicamp. The fact that five of the Jets' first six picks in that spring's draft, including me, were linebackers or defensive linemen spoke volumes about where they considered themselves weakest. Those other four picks were there when I arrived: Marvin Washington, a defensive end out of Idaho; Ron Stallworth, another DE out of Auburn; Joe Mott, a linebacker from Iowa; and my roommate for the next six weeks, Jeff Lageman.

Camp was tough, but when they announced the final roster, I was on it, along with six other defensive linemen. This was my family now, a group of men I would get to know better than anyone in my life besides my wife, parents, brothers, and sisters.

It didn't matter to me that I wasn't a starter—and I wasn't. I began the season where I'd begun with Tulsa, on the kickoff and punt teams, with the first kickoff of my regular season career coming in Giants Stadium against the New England Patriots. The feeling was the same as I'd had in college, too, a mixture of exhilaration and dread. I don't know anyone who's ever been on a kickoff team who's not been either absolutely horrified or a complete lunatic. The best are a mixture of both.

I played some backup on the line and was hungry for my first sack, starving for it. A sack is the milestone by which a defensive lineman is judged. It means you've not only beaten the guy you're rushing against but the quarterback as well. To me, a sack has always been the ultimate high in football. It's hard to describe that feeling when you've got a quarterback in your hands, when you take him down and the crowd goes crazy and your teammates mob you. It's just like a score. Touchdowns, sacks, long interception returns—these are the things people come to see. Just like the home run in baseball. That's what a sack is—the defensive lineman's home run.

I came close in Cleveland in our second game of the season. I bashed Bernie Kosar three times, just after he threw the ball. I came up blank the next two weeks against the Dolphins and the Colts. Then, finally, I got the first sack of my career against Jay Schroeder and the Raiders, and it couldn't have come at a better time—Monday night.

There really is something special about a Monday night game. That's when the pomp comes out and the spotlight is on. Every other player in the league is tuned in, which means, among other things, that Monday night is where you pick up a lot of your Pro Bowl votes.

Monday nights are special for fans, too. To this day, people come up to me and say, "Oh, man, I saw that hit you put on Schroeder on Monday night." As if it happened last week.

That year I had seven sacks, one short of the Jets' record. I made the All-Rookie team, too. But the Jets ended up 4–12, the worst record in the AFC. I wanted to turn that around.

8

An Avalanche
of Injuries

I had been through a lot of shifting in my life,
lots of transition, but none more than in 1990. And all
the changes that year were for the better. In many
ways, this was probably the best year of my life.

It began when Angela and I found our first home,
the first and only house we've ever owned.

Next, the Jets had a new coach: Bruce Coslet.
There was one more change too: I became a father.
Little Ashtin, the joy of my life, arrived on July 11.

With Bruce Coslet came a new defensive coordinator, Pete Carroll. He had coached at Minnesota

before joining the Jets. With the Vikings, he'd built a mobile, attacking, speed-oriented 4–3 defense anchored by a tackle in the middle who more or less "floated" from side to side, keying off the other team's guards. Carroll called this position the "Eagle" tackle. It was the key to his entire defensive scheme, and it required a player who was a blend of both linebacker and defensive end, a player who had both the size and the athleticism to roam the line, find the gaps, and burst through to close on the quarterback. At Minnesota, that player had been Keith Millard, who flourished under Carroll's system, becoming an All-Pro and the league's Defensive Player of the Year. The season before, Millard had led the league with 18 sacks.

Now Carroll had brought his system to New York, and the player he was relying on to make it work was me.

I was elated. I had started the final five games the season before, and now I was going to be out there from the beginning, playing the kind of position I was born for.

Greg Robinson, our defensive line coach, summed it up pretty succinctly early that training camp. "We're just gonna put you in the middle," he said, "and turn you loose." Sounded good to me.

Unfortunately, it wasn't to be a great season: 6–10. But we knew we were going places.

We came into the 1991 season with something the Jets hadn't had in a while—momentum. Our defense had upped its sack total the year before by ten (from 28 my rookie year to 38 in '90), and even more was expected from us now. Our line was still basically a young group of kids, growing every game. Jeff had been switched from linebacker to end, and he was still getting untracked. Marvin had yet to become the impact player I knew he could be. And I wasn't satisfied with the success I'd had in 1990. It meant nothing if our team wasn't winning football games.

The New York press was now comparing our line to the old "Sack Exchange," calling us "The Byrdmen of the Meadowlands." They were counting on me to be the leader. One columnist wrote, "This is the player who will supplant Lawrence Taylor as New York's most feared pass rusher, maybe even this year."

That was going a little far, but I did have high hopes, both for the team and for myself.

What I wound up facing on the field was the same situation I'd seen in high school and college. There's a Japanese saying for it that I recently heard: "The nail that sticks out gets hammered." I was that nail. I was being double- and triple-teamed now on every play. Tampa Bay, Seattle, Buffalo, Chicago . . . game after game it was the same, two or three guys being thrown my way—someone sliding down the line and maybe a running back tossed in for good measure. I was getting

the fire beat out of me, taking a pounding. After nine games I had just two sacks, and the same reporters who had been comparing me to LT were now writing me off. "Byrd has pretty much laid an egg this year" was the way one described it.

I wasn't ecstatic, but I understood what was happening. I knew all that attention on me meant my teammates were now freer to step up and deliver. That's what the coaches were telling them they had to do, and they did. Through those same nine games, Marvin had six sacks and Jeff had four. Most importantly, we were now a winning team. By mid-November, we were 6–5 and aiming at the play-offs.

That's when a tragedy happened in Detroit that swept through the league like a shock wave. Mike Utley broke his neck. I was in the locker room getting changed when Bob Reese, our trainer, came up and told me Utley had hurt himself against the Rams at the Silverdome. I asked him how serious it was, and Bob said word was he was paralyzed from his chest down.

I couldn't believe it. When you think of injuries, even bad ones, you think of knees and shoulders. You never imagine a broken neck. I'd seen one broken neck in my career, and it was one of the most unsettling experiences of my life.

I prayed a lot for Mike that month. The whole league was rocked by what happened to him. And the

Lions became a team on a mission, playing on incredible emotion. They tore through us 34–20. They tore through everyone until the Redskins finally stopped them one game short of the Super Bowl, in the NFC championship. That's what Mike meant to the guys who loved him.

Meanwhile, we had our own mission to focus on. We went into the last game of the season head-to-head against Miami for the AFC's last wild card play-off berth. The Dolphins were waiting for us in Joe Robbie Stadium, knowing the winner of that game was in and the loser was out. We put a new wrinkle in that afternoon, slipping me out to left end, and it worked. I had six tackles that day, along with two-and-a-half sacks off Marino, and we beat the Dolphins 23–20 in overtime for the sweetest win of my professional career. For the first time in five years, the Jets were in the play-offs.

That was the highlight of that season, meeting Warren Moon and the Oilers in the Astrodome, in one of the AFC's two wild card games.

This day, our coaches tried yet another wrinkle, geared to Houston's run-and-shoot offense. They slanted me into the teeth of the Oilers' pass protection, inviting a double-team and counting on our linebackers to then rush the gaps.

It didn't work. At least, it didn't work well

enough. We lost 17–10, and another season was through. We couldn't wait for the next one to start.

By then I was more deeply involved in my faith than ever, not only in New York, where our Wednesday night Bible study group had become a foundation of our life, but back home in Oklahoma as well, where Angela and I were both extremely active in speaking to schools, to youth groups, and to churches. I'd been coming back to Mustang since I left for college, to our church and to the high school, keeping in touch with the kids there, letting them know what being a Christian had meant to my life. Now I was doing it not just there but across the state and in some of the surrounding midwestern states as well. Angela and I sang and spoke to youth groups in homes, churches, and under tents all over Oklahoma, Texas, and Colorado. We had always felt a special bond to teenagers and children, and now that I'd become a professional athlete, we were using the opportunities that God gave us to witness even more.

I was eager to get the next season started. And when it did, I arrived in camp that year with a Mohawk haircut, something to get the guys' juices flowing. Mers said he liked it so much he was thinking of getting one himself.

I'd never seen the team so loose, and it showed. We went undefeated in the preseason, winning five games, and our defense was stellar. I even scored my first touchdown as a Jet, a seven-yard interception return against Philadelphia on a ball thrown by my old buddy Jeff Kemp.

There was no reason to be overly worried when we lost our regular season opener in Atlanta, no reason to suspect that when our first-round draft pick, tight end Johnny Mitchell, went out that day with a separated shoulder, it would be the first of what would become a season-long avalanche of injuries. No reason to fear that what we figured to be a dream year was about to turn into a nightmare.

We lost the second game, too, against Pittsburgh. Worse, Jeff blew out his knee hitting Neil O'Donnell, the Steelers' quarterback. The way Jeff lay there holding his leg when that play was done, I knew it was bad. When I got back to the sidelines, I asked Jeff if he was going to be okay. He said they told him he was done for the year. My heart stopped. Losing him like that was a huge shock to the team.

Marvin stepped into Jeff's spot and did a great job, but you could feel it in the air. The year before we hadn't had hardly an injury to speak of, but now our guys suddenly seemed to be dropping like flies. Hamstrings, shoulders, ankles, ribs, knees, feet, groins, backs, fingers, thumbs—before the season was through, twenty-two of our players would miss a total of 109 games. That included eleven starters.

Including me. I went down in game four, against

the Rams in Los Angeles. It was the middle of the second quarter, and I had beaten their right offensive guard, Number 71. Jim Everett stepped up, and as I dove at his legs, I stretched out my right arm to reach for him and hit the turf, popping out my shoulder.

Now, for the first time in my career, I had to watch my teammates from the sidelines. I'd never missed a regular season game. Not in high school, not in college.

The next four weeks were killers, watching from the sidelines with that separated shoulder as we beat New England for our first win of the year—we got seven sacks in that game, and all I could do was lick my chops—then we lost to Indianapolis and Buffalo.

It actually looked like things might take a turn for the better when I came back for the Miami game at home the first week in November. The Dolphins were 6–1, tied with the Bills for the AFC East lead, but our defense dominated them that day. I had no numbers to speak of, no sacks or tackles, but I was breathing down Marino's neck most of the afternoon.

The next week we went to Denver, where Al Toon, one of the best receivers in the league, a Pro Bowler, went down with a concussion, and we went down 27–16. We came back with a win against Cincinnati at home, then got hammered at New England.

I dragged home that evening about midnight, feeling as low as I could remember. We were 3–8 and we'd just been pounded by the Patriots, who hadn't won a game that season until the week before. When I came through the door, there was Ashtin. She often stayed up late like that on Sundays, waiting for me to get in.

I picked her up and carried her over to the sofa. Ange sat down beside us, and we started talking about this whole year, how awful it had been losing Jeff, my hurting my shoulder, and the team doing so poorly. Just sitting there like that was wonderful. I felt so good that night, knowing I had my wife and my little girl, holding them both in my arms.

We had Kansas City to think about Sunday.

I'd always played well against the Chiefs, against that offense. I'd always gotten a few sacks against them, which was just what I needed since I hadn't had one yet all year. I had started referring to myself as His Royal Sacklessness, and I couldn't wait to drop that title.

The morning of the game, I was up at 8:15, same as always. The whole team had breakfast in the hotel restaurant, then Bruce got up and gave his thoughts about the game.

Time passed. We warmed up. Finally, it was time to play.

"Bring it in!" Bruce called, and everyone came together. We said the Lord's Prayer in unison. Then a moment of silence. Then a simple sentence from Bruce: "Let's go get 'em, fellas."

There's nothing like that feeling of sprinting out onto a football field at game time, emerging from the darkness of a stadium tunnel into the light of a Sunday afternoon, the sound of your echoing footsteps and the muted roar of the crowd replaced by the blast of 57,000 fans rocking the very air you breathe. If you've got any fire in you at all, it's flaming by then.

We won the toss and received. Three plays, Louie came in to punt, then it was time for our defense. The Chiefs did what we expected, running Word and Okoye mostly off the guards. We nailed them pretty well that first series, mostly for just one- and two-yard gains. Dave Krieg had to throw the ball, which was what we wanted. But Krieg started out hot, hitting his first four passes, and they came away from that first series with a field goal. They got another at the start of the second quarter, and that's where we were at the half, down 6–0.

I remember Greg Robinson, our defensive line coach, coming up to me and saying the pressure was going good. I was getting by Rich Valerio, the Chiefs right tackle, a lot. "Just keep it up," Greg told me. "You're gonna get there."

The Chiefs took the second half kickoff at the west end of the stadium and returned it to their 25. First down Krieg rolled my way and threw a quick sideline pass.

Incomplete.

Second and ten.

They broke their huddle, came to the line, and I knew it was a pass by the way Valerio was set. There was the down, too. And the yardage. And their position on the field. Everything said it was going to be a pass.

I remember adjusting outside just a touch. I was counting on Krieg taking a deep drop, seven steps. On the snap, I came right at Valerio, then chopped him and slid around the outside. There's always a point in the pass rush where you know you've got the guy beat, and I'd reached that point. I'd beaten Valerio cleanly.

I remember coming around the corner, leaning in and lowering my shoulder to keep Valerio from getting back on me. You plant everything low at a point like that, dipping your body and driving with everything you've got, turning that corner at top speed.

I could see Krieg right then, his white jersey filling my field of vision. He was actually above the spot I expected, which was great. That's just how you want it. But then he stepped up.

Krieg must have seen me, too. Or sensed me. Typically, a quarterback will set up at the back of the pocket and let the offensive tackle ride an outside-rushing defensive end on by. But Krieg, seeing I was bearing down on him so fast, knew that the only way out for him was to step up.

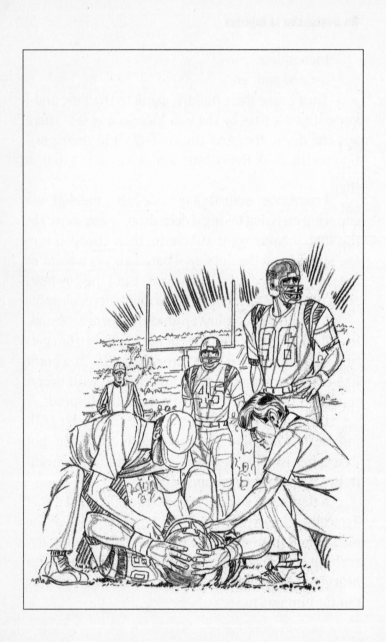

My momentum and sheer centrifugal force were slinging me out even as I was straining to lean in. At this point I knew I was not going to be able to tackle Krieg, so I chopped at the football with my right arm as I came past. I remember focusing on that football, bringing my hand down, actually hitting it, and then.... In an instant, in the millisecond it takes to bat an eye, something rose in front of me like a wall. A huge green wall, inches from my face, my body hurtling through the air with all its might.

All my years of training, the thousands of tackles I'd made, the way I'd been taught to hit with my head up, to keep that spine bent so it can take a blow, all that meant nothing at that instant. I wasn't making a tackle. My reaction wasn't that of a football player. It was an instinctual reaction, the reaction anyone would have when they're suddenly about to slam into something head-on and they've got a thousandth of a second to respond.

I ducked.

I ducked my head instead of raising it up. I hunched my shoulders, pulling in my head, all in an instant.

I felt a solid thump. And everything slowed down.

Everything fell away.

Then everything stopped.

9

The Halo Vest

I still had my uniform on, from helmet to shoulder pads to shoes, as the ambulance pulled out from beneath Giants Stadium. My body was lashed down from head to toe. All I could move were my eyes. But I could hear the siren as we lurched into traffic, racing toward Manhattan's Lenox Hill Hospital. Pepper Burruss was gripping my helmet as Steve Nicholas sliced off my wrist tape and the tape around my shoes and ankles, then slipped off my gloves, shoes, and socks. He cut open my pants and jersey, then sliced open my shoulder pads. He could see I was having trouble breathing.

I could sense Steve fiddling with my feet. I could feel the pressure of something being laid across my legs.

"I can feel that!" I exclaimed. "Is that good? Is that a good sign?"

He didn't answer.

I could hear the driver commenting how lucky we were that the lanes weren't as crowded as usual for a Sunday afternoon. Every time I was touched, from an IV line being put into my arm to my uniform being sliced, I made a point that I could feel it. I was trying to convince Steve, and trying to convince myself, that everything was going to be all right.

My mind raced to Mike Utley.

"Was Mike able to feel anything?" I asked. "Is this what it was like for Mike?"

No answer.

Ange must have told me she loved me a hundred times, over and over and over again. She tried kissing my face but couldn't because of the mask. Pepper cut my chin strap then tried unscrewing the mask, but the grommets wouldn't budge.

I wasn't thinking about football anymore. For the first time, I asked a question that would become the focal point of my entire life in the months to come. "Steve," I said, "am I going to be able to walk again?"

His answer was dead honest, one I would hear repeated by every doctor I dealt with.

"Dennis," he said, "I don't know."

I looked toward Angela, who was leaning over me, keeping herself in my field of vision.

"Ange, I don't care about football," I said. "All I want now is to be able to hold you and Ashtin. That's all I care about."

Her eyes were wet with tears as she put her face as close to mine as she could, gripping my left hand and stroking it.

"Don't worry," she said. "We'll hold you."

Then we prayed, Pepper and Ange and I. There were trials ahead of me that I could not imagine, so many moments where my faith and strength would be tested, but nothing would be more crucial than the prayer we shared inside that ambulance. Because it was then and there that I found the inner core of peace that would see me through everything to come. At that moment, en route to the hospital, I turned everything over to the Lord.

We were only in that ambulance forty minutes before it pulled up to the emergency room doors of Lenox Hill on East 77th Street. Just before we got there, it occurred to me to ask a question I'd normally ask immediately after a play like the one that had put me here. "Ange," I said, "did I get the sack?"

Then the doors opened and everything began whirling around me. People passing on the sidewalk stopped and looked as I was lifted out of the ambulance then rolled through Lenox Hill's emergency room doors. As they pushed me inside, I felt as though I was in every hospital movie I'd ever seen, the patient lying on his back, the lights and ceiling tiles flashing by, the gurney being wheeled around one corner then another, the IV lines connected to the bottles of clear fluid, all swaying above me as we rushed into the emergency room. Ange was taken away and told to wait.

No sooner was I wheeled into a room for X-rays than Pepper had a cast cutter in his hands.

There were four grommets attaching the mask to the helmet and Pepper had to cut off each one. Chips and dust flew from the saw and covered my face. Finally, Pepper was able to pull off the mask. Then, very gently, as carefully as if they were handling an egg, Steve and Pepper lifted my head slightly and slid off the helmet. Pepper kept my head suspended as Steve cut off the rest of my jersey and took off my shoulder pads. The rest of my clothing came off, too.

By now the IVs were pumping steroids into my veins to stem the swelling in my spinal cord. There was no telling yet about the extent of damage to that ropy bundle of nerves—whether it had been bruised or even torn to some degree—but it was critical to keep the swelling down as much as possible in these first hours because swelling can put pressure on the nerves to the point of damaging them permanently.

Steroids cut the swelling, but they also wrack the body with nausea. And I was being pumped full of the stuff. Within fifteen minutes of the first dose I started throwing up. Vomit was just bubbling out of my mouth, running all over Pepper's and Steve's arms and hands. I couldn't turn my head to empty my mouth and I couldn't blow it out because my insides were paralyzed, too. I didn't have the muscle strength to even blow my nose. There was no way I could spit out this vomit.

So Pepper and Steve had to take care of it. Each time I was about to heave, I would tell them, and gently, ever so slightly, they would roll my body to one side and let the vomit run out of my mouth onto their hands and arms.

Next step was the X-rays. But they showed nothing.

After that, they rushed me to the third floor for a CAT scan—a three-dimensional X-ray of the head—and that's where they saw it: The fifth cervical vertebra at the base of my neck was fractured. Now they could see what they already knew. My neck was broken.

About 11:30 P.M., with my friends gone and only Angela and Pepper still with me, I was wheeled out once again, this time into a room filled with beeping equipment and a bank of bright lights overhead. I was lying there studying the hinges on those lights when a technician leaned over and told me what we were waiting for.

"The doctors will be here soon," he said. "They're going to put your halo vest on."

A halo vest.

My mind flashed to Marcus Anderson, my teammate at Tulsa who had broken his neck. I'd watched him live in a halo vest for six months. He had to sleep in a La-Z-Boy chair that whole time. He couldn't lie down in a bed. I could still see him cleaning the screws that came out of his head. Every day he had to clean his screws.

And now they were going to put screws in me. Now they were going to put a halo vest on me. Once more I had to gather the strength to stay calm. Once more I prayed for the Lord to help me.

The first thing they did was mark four spots, two on the edges of my forehead and two at the back of my skull. Then the anesthesiologist gave me a shot of xylocane at each of those spots. Then they simply began screwing.

I remember the metal pins crunching through my skin. Not squeaking. Crunching. Each screw is stainless steel, about a quarter-inch in diameter, and they really had to push to get them through the skin and then into my skull. They had to push hard, so hard that one of them was on the other side pushing back.

All this pushing, all this pressure was frightening. I imagined the force it takes to twist a screw into a piece of wood, and I realized these men were using that same force to twist these pieces of steel into my head. I imagined the bone separating, splitting open like a piece of pine. I knew that wasn't happening, but that's how it felt. The thought of Frankenstein even crossed my mind.

Then it was done, the screws were in, and they pulled out the vest, a plastic shell shaped like the chest armor worn by Roman centurions. The inside was lined with sheep's wool to keep it from abrading my chest.

They put me in that, cinching it down so tightly I wasn't sure I could breathe. Breathing was hard enough already. The doctors were keeping an eye on my breathing, worried I might need a respirator, as so many spinal injury patients do. And now I had this vest adding to that feeling of constriction. That feeling alone was frightening enough, and I had no idea if I'd be wearing it for six weeks or six months, like Marcus.

Or longer.

Finally they connected four metal rods from the vest to each of the screws, did some tightening, tossed the tools in a little pouch connected to my vest, made a joke about the tool chest I was wearing, and that was it. My head was locked, totally immobile.

My field of vision was framed on the sides by two metal bars.

It was 1:00 A.M. Now, at last, this day was over. Ange was there as they laid me in bed. It was close to three before I finally fell asleep, haunted by a question that would wake me up in the middle of many nights to come.

Was this really happening to me?

10

The Red Beret

When I opened my eyes Monday morning, a steady parade of nurses and doctors streamed into the room, checking the machinery and the tubes, taking tests, asking me questions, marking charts, tapping on my toes, my feet, my knees with small probes and hammers. Among them was a fairly tall man with horn rim glasses and a pleasant Irish brogue—Dr. O'Leary. He explained what had happened, what they'd done and why—that I'd been stabilized in the halo vest and that they were waiting for the swelling to go down before they operated to repair the damage. The operation, he told me, would be Wednesday.

What he couldn't tell me was what I most wanted to know. Would I be able to walk again? What were my chances? No one could tell me. The answer was always "We don't know. . . ." Not "I don't know," but "We don't know," as if that somehow relieved them of the onus of responsibility.

There is a verse in the Bible that I had gathered strength from many times in my life, and I would turn to it many more times in the coming months. It's in the book of Matthew, where Jesus is in the Garden of Gethsemane, deeply distressed by the weakness of Peter and the betrayal of Judas. His soul is torn by the pain closing in around him, and he falls to his knees and prays: "My Father, if it is possible, may this cup be taken from me. Yet, not as I will, but as you will."

I went to sleep Monday night thinking of those words.

Tuesday, the doctors gathered Angela, my parents, and Rick Schaeffer, who is my agent, lawyer, and good friend. They said that beyond the steroids they'd already started and the surgery that was set for the next morning, there was an experimental drug they were considering, a drug called Sygen.

Sygen is aimed at doing something researchers into spinal cord injuries not long ago thought impossible—rescuing and regenerating damaged nerve cells. It's made from molecules located in the outer membrane layer of central nervous system cells in humans and other mammals.

The doctors talked to me about the drug, explaining its untested nature, what it might be able to do, and the question of side effects. The decision to use Sygen was totally up to Angela and me, but we had to decide soon because for Sygen to be effective, treatment has to begin within seventy-two hours of the injury. It had already been forty-eight. The clock was ticking. If we were going to start it, it had to be the next day.

In my mind, there was no question. This was a no-brainer. The possibility of side effects didn't compare to the promise of what this drug might do for me. "Let's do it," I said. Angela guided my hand as we scrawled a mark that passed for my signature. So now there was one more item to add to the list for Wednesday's surgery: Start the Sygen.

Only my family, Rick Schaeffer, and the doctors knew anything about this decision. The friends and teammates still streaming in to visit me had no idea.

Marvin came by that afternoon. He stayed about twenty minutes, and before he left, he leaned down and whispered in my ear.

"Dennis," he said, "the Lord wouldn't give you this cross if you couldn't bear it."

Marvin always had a knack for saying the right thing at the right time.

Then, for the first time since we'd collided, Scott came through the door. I'd thought a lot about Scott, and I was worried about him. I imagined he might be feeling some guilt that somehow he was partly responsible for what had happened.

I knew Scott well. He was one of the biggest, strongest men I'd ever played with—he'd been runner-up in the NFL Strongest Man competition in '88. But Scott also had a sensitive side. He responded emotionally to many things, and I knew he had to be hurting right now.

He hadn't realized it was me he'd collided with down on that field any more than I'd known it was he. He didn't even know what had hit him. All he knew was that he was bent backwards by the blow, badly twisting his ankle underneath him and blasting the air out of his lungs. It was only after his cobwebs had cleared and he was being helped off the field that he saw someone else lying on the turf.

"Who is that?" he'd asked.

There was definitely some tension on his face when he looked in my hospital room door. But whatever questions he might have had about how I felt toward him vanished as soon as our eyes met. I was so glad to see him, and I showed it. When he saw me beaming at him like that, he just lit up. He was Scotty again.

He came over and hugged me then showed me something he'd brought. It was a paratrooper's beret.

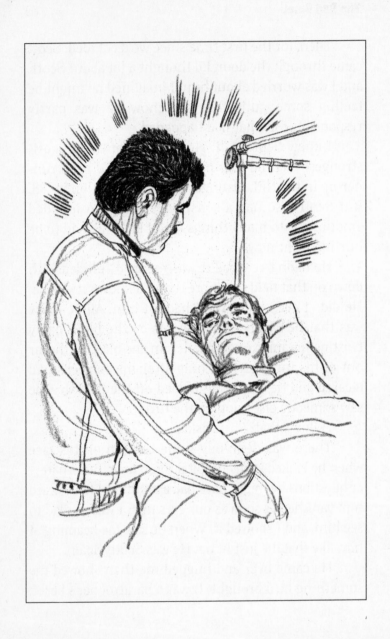

Scott's accountant, a man named Craig Northacker, had spent four years as a paratrooper with the 82nd Airborne Division in Fort Bragg, North Carolina. He'd watched men die after jumping out of airplanes. He'd seen guys wind up in wheelchairs. He'd hurt himself so badly on the last jump of his career—a night jump—that it took him three years to heal. He'd given Scott this red beret to pass on to me as a symbol of the courage and bravery he'd seen among the men he'd served with.

I was really touched. I'd always had enormous respect for men who had served in combat. That beret was going to stay with me a long time.

"Hey," I finally said, "I really blasted you, didn't I?"

Scott reared back, as if he'd stuck his finger in a socket.

"Dennis, I can't believe you said that! I was going to wait till you got a little better, then I was going to tell you exactly the same thing. You knocked it out of me. I swear, you hit me harder than anyone ever hit me in my life."

That was it. We broke up laughing, and I could tell a load had been lifted off both of us.

Finally night fell. Tuesday night. Angela's dad and Pastor McNabb from our church in Mustang had arrived and had come by to see me, but now everyone was gone but Angela.

It had been less than three days since the hit, but

already it seemed a lifetime ago. I was exhausted. And anxious. And uncertain. The next morning would be my moment of truth. That surgery would set the course for the rest of my life. I had no idea what the doctors would find in there. They didn't either. They couldn't. Almost everything I wanted to know about my condition brought the same basic answer: "We'll have to wait and see." It was the same with the surgery.

Angela and I talked about the surgery and how I felt about the decisions we'd made. I felt fine, I told her. Then I told her something else. "Ange," I said, "I'm glad God chose me for this because he knows I have the strength and faith to get through it."

Ange leaned down in tears and hugged me. "I'm glad, too," she said. "I'm glad God chose me to go through it with you."

Then she left. And I turned my thoughts toward the next day. I knew better than to expect a miracle. I knew I would never play football again. That was over. But walking—being well again—I found myself imagining that. That somehow with this surgery, the wires would suddenly start firing again, that I'd wake up after this operation and my limbs would be back.

I was hoping for that.

11

Seven-Hour Surgery

Seven hours. That's how long I laid on the operating table that Wednesday as the doctors opened my neck and got a firsthand look at what until then they had been able to see only through X-ray machines—my shattered spine.

The procedure went "perfectly," according to Dr. Caimans. He said he'd gotten up for this surgery the way an athlete gets up for a ball game. Going in, he felt the same sort of tension and adrenaline I did before a kickoff. He'd had to prepare himself physically as well as mentally, as had the whole six-surgeon team. Seven hours is a long time.

But it had gone off without a hitch. Blessedly, the halo vest was off. They'd removed it during the procedure, an indication of how stable my neck was now with plates in it. It was a fantastic relief having that halo off. I could move my head now by tilting it from side to side. Now I just had to put up with a soft neck collar. I felt pain from the stitches front and back, but that was all right. This was a step. I was excited, eager. Okay, I thought, I've got that out of the way. What's next?

The same questions came flooding out again. When will I be able to sit up? Hold my children? Hunt? When will I be able to walk? Again, no answers. The doctors' concerns were more immediate. They were monitoring my liver enzymes, watching my blood pressure and other vital signs, and checking a dozen other charts only they understood.

None of the doctors told me I'd never walk again, but I could tell some of them thought it. They couldn't help but think it.

Elliott Hershman, the Jets' head physician, was the only doctor who gave an honest reply to my question, "Will I be able to walk again?"

"It could be years before we know," he said, looking through his round, owlish glasses.

Years. That word hit me as hard as my collision with Scott. I appreciated Dr. Hershman's honesty more than I could ever say. But those words were hard to hear. Years before they'd even know if I could walk? The fantasies I'd had the night before evaporated like so much steam.

Late that day, I finally found out who got the sack on that life-changing play.

Throughout the years, Scott and I would often fight and argue over who should have gotten this sack or that. When two guys hit a quarterback close to the same time, there's often a gray area about who gets the credit. Scott was always telling me I was stealing his sacks and vice versa.

That's how it went with this one. They originally gave Scott credit for sacking Krieg on the play that put me down. But after looking at the films, the Jets petitioned the league to change the ruling. That Thursday, they did. Greg Robinson came by to tell me the news.

So I had my first sack of the year—and the last of my career. Funny how my four years as a pro began with a sack against Kansas City—in that preseason game my rookie season—and ended with a sack against the same team.

12

A Toe Moves

I continued to get more calls than they could count at the hospital's switchboard. The hospital staff worked that Friday evening to rig up a phone system with a headset I could wear to make it easier to handle the calls. I could answer the phone by pushing my head against a pad laid on my pillow, then I listened through a speaker and talked through the headset microphone.

I was trying it out that night with my sisters, who had had a terrible time trying to get through to me, when suddenly one of the hospital operators cut in and told me Bill Clinton was on another line, waiting to speak to me.

Right. Ha ha. "Could you tell him I'm on the line with my sisters?" I said. And I went back to our call. I didn't give the Clinton thing a second thought. I'd been getting crank calls all week from people telling the operator they were teammates or friends or someone famous, so they could get through.

A minute later my dad came in with a small card in his hand. "Son," he said, "that really was the president . . . or the president-elect. He left this number."

I couldn't believe it. I called the number right away—my dad dialed it for me—and sure enough, a secretary came on the line, and in a couple of seconds I was talking to Bill Clinton.

"Hi, Dennis," he said. "I wanted to call and tell you I've been thinking a lot about you lately. And I want you to know I'm praying for you."

"Thank you very much," I said. "I'm praying for you, too. The way things are going, you need it more than I do."

I didn't really know what to say. I mean, what do you say to the president of the United States? Especially on the spur of the moment. We talked for about ten minutes. I told him I'd never talked to a president before, and he told me he hadn't talked to many football players. He knew Keith Jackson, he said, since Jackson's from Arkansas. But that's about it.

Finally he wished me luck. "I wish *you* luck," I said. "You're the one who's inherited the problems."

*   *   *

It was early the next morning, Saturday morning, that I did something I hadn't done since being carried off the field the Sunday before. I moved my toes.

It actually had happened for the first time on Thursday, just a microscopic movement, a flick in my right big toe. Steve Nicholas had been there and thought he saw it, too. But I couldn't reproduce it, I couldn't make it happen again, so the doctors wrote it off as an involuntary reflex, a withdrawal response, although Steve maintained it was genuine.

By Friday, though, I could feel the impulses inside the toes of my right foot. I couldn't move anything, but I told Steve I could feel the nerves firing. Something was happening down there. There was no doubt about it. This was not the totally dead feeling I'd had up till then.

Saturday the doctors saw it. It was about 7:30 in the morning, and Dr. O'Leary was giving me the once-over, asking me the usual questions, pushing and poking me in the usual places, telling me to try and move this, try and move that. Finally, he came to my right foot. He asked me to try to move the toes, which I did. And, suddenly, almost imperceptibly, the big toe ... moved. You could hardly see it. It was like the flick of an eyelash. But it definitely moved.

Dr. O'Leary asked me to do it again to make sure

I was doing it on my own. Then again. Then he went through the ceiling. "It's a miracle!" he shouted. And he was out the door, racing down the hall to make some phone calls. Steve Nicholas was across the hall, examining a ninety-four-year-old man with a hip fracture. He came over to see what all the fuss was about. "Hey, bud," I said. "Watch this." And I wiggled the toe.

Steve couldn't believe it. He was ecstatic. He had his right hand on the top of my foot and this big grin on his face.

"So is this good?" I asked.

"Good?" he said. "If you had done this two months from now, we would have been thrilled." Steve rushed out to call Bob Reese over at the Jets complex, where the team would be coming in soon for morning practice before leaving for Buffalo, where we'd be playing the Bills Sunday.

I dialed Angela, who was at the hotel with Mindi Blanchard, teammate Cary Blanchard's wife. They were getting set to come over about ten. I asked her how she was doing, what was going on. We chatted for a couple of minutes, then she asked me what was happening here.

"Oh, nothing much," I said. "I moved my toe this morning."

She went crazy, screaming and yelling. She hung up the phone and rushed right over. By the time she and Mindi got there, I was moving the foot itself, just a hair.

That entire week, from the moment I had arrived at the hospital, I had resolved that I was going to let what had happened to me be a witness for the Lord, that I was going to let this tragedy be a blessing to other people's lives through my strength and perseverance. I knew I had to trust in the Lord, and that's what I did. That's what I prayed for—strength and wisdom and courage.

Then that toe moved. And the moment it did, I knew what I had to do now. I knew my calling. I knew I had to do more than accept and work with what I'd been left with. I knew I had to take my body back. Once that toe moved, then the quad, I spent every waking moment training all my willpower, all my physical and mental strength, on those two places in my body, straining to fan those faint little flickers into something more. I'd lie there flexing that quad over and over and over until it was so fatigued I couldn't flex any more. I did the same with my toe. I couldn't touch it; I couldn't even see it, but I could lie there looking up at the ceiling and put every ounce of effort, my whole being, into that right big toe.

The way the guys felt about all this news they could have flown up to Buffalo without the plane. I thought a lot about them that afternoon and about the game. After you spend four years getting conditioned to a certain routine, it's hard to shake it quickly. I wasn't on the plane with my teammates, but I had Buffalo on my mind, just as they did.

What stood out most that Sunday morning, though, was seeing Joe Namath walk into my room. I'd met Joe Namath my rookie year. We were playing the Rams in Anaheim, and I was out on the field early as usual, testing it with my cleats. I was down around the south end zone, looking up the field, when I felt a hand on my shoulder and heard a voice. "Hello, Dennis," he said as I turned around. "I'm Joe Namath."

All I could think was, *Holy smokes, this is Joe Namath!* I towered over him, and yet I felt like a kid standing next to a giant. Broadway Joe. He was the same figure to me that he was to every kid—a legend, bigger than life. I couldn't believe he had walked up and was talking to me. And he knew my name! Now he was here in my hospital room, and I was dumbstruck again. Sure, I was a professional athlete myself. There were trading cards with my picture on them sold in stores. People asked for my autograph when I went out to eat. But Joe Namath, Joe DiMaggio—these guys are the best-known sports figures in the world. And here was Namath, visiting me. He shuffled in with his hands in his pockets, almost shy. He'd waited for everyone else to be gone. He just wanted to visit a little bit by himself.

I remember saying to him that he probably knew

hospitals pretty well, since he'd been in a few himself. That broke the ice, and he started telling me about hurting his famous knee for the first time back in 1965, the year before I was born. Then he told me how Jim Nicholas's mother Julia had given him a St. Jude's medal just before Jim operated on his knee. He said he wore that medal during every game after that. He had kept it ever since.

And now he took it off and handed it toward me. "I want you to have this," he said. I raised my head up, and he slipped the medal around my neck. He was incredibly solemn about what he was doing. I could tell he was really moved. And so was I. I vowed to myself that medal would stay around my neck from then on.

Then it was back to the game in Buffalo. I'd missed the pregame prayer the Buffalo crowd had had for me, the moment of silence before the national anthem, and the TV cameras showing a plane flying over Rich Stadium pulling a banner that read "Get Well Dennis Byrd."

I could see the guys were wearing the Ichthus I always wore on my shoes and my number on their helmets, and I could see some of the Bills wearing it, too! I was overcome. As much as we had this intense war in the trenches, as much as we battled each other between those sidelines, those guys were still able to show the brotherhood they felt with me. They really had class.

We were ahead 17–10 when the fourth quarter began. I'd been down on that field so many times, I could almost feel it, lying there in that hospital bed, the wind whistling over that frozen turf, the cold cutting you to the core, the deafening roar of 76,000 Bills fans. The gusts were blowing forty-five miles an hour that afternoon, pulling the temperature on the field down to three below zero. Snow was piled on the sidelines, as it usually is in Buffalo in December.

It felt so familiar. So did the touchdown pass Kelly threw five minutes into that final quarter, tying the game at seventeen, which is where the score was when the Bills got the ball on their own nineteen with just under two minutes to go. That felt familiar, too. I couldn't help thinking, *Here we go again*. The clock ticking down. Kelly driving them up the field. It had happened like that so many times.

But not this time.

On second down from his eighteen, Kelly lofted a pass to the left sideline, toward his wide receiver, James Lofton. He never saw Brian Washington, our safety on that side. I couldn't even raise my arms as Bee-Dub— that's short for "BW"—cut in front of that pass and took it in for the score. I couldn't jump up and cheer the way I wanted to as I watched Marvin there in the end zone, waving toward the camera, waving toward me, flashing the signal I always gave Ange from the sidelines, the thumb, forefinger, and pinkie extended on one hand, sign language for "I love you." I couldn't leap up the way I wanted to, but I was dancing as I lay there in that bed. I was dancing.

And when Bill Pickel threw Kelly down with a minute to go, stripped the ball, and fell on the fumble, I cried.

And then it was over. We'd won. Incredibly, we'd won.

Less than four hours later, Steve Gutman, the Jets' president, came into my room along with Jim Nicholas and Pete and Greg. They'd flown straight back from Buffalo, and they had the game ball with them. There'd been no doubt about who should have it, they said.

I'd earned three game balls during my career with the Jets, but none of them would ever be as special as this one.

So that's how that day ended. The curtain had come down on a week that was probably more trying than any this football team had ever been through. My teammates had pulled off a miracle that afternoon.

Now it was time to turn back to fighting and praying for a miracle of my own. Jesus Christ had been with me during the past ten days more than he had ever been with me in my entire life.

I knew I would need him even more in the days ahead.

13

Rehab

The next step for me was rehabilitation. I was moved to Mount Sinai hospital, and it began. The first day I was wheeled into the rehab room, I realized I was entering a world different from anything I'd ever known, filled with men and women who were just like I was now—severely physically disabled.

A lot of people worked with me while I was at Mount Sinai, but the two most important ones were Lawrence Harding, my physical therapist, and Joanne Giammetta, my occupational therapist. Joanne is a tiny little woman, but she has enormous energy. She became what my brothers had been for me when I was growing up—both my shepherd and my slave driver. She made it clear that I would have to *work* here, at least five hours a day, six days a week. That was fine with me.

The first thing they had to do was get me up and into a chair. That in itself was torture. Since I'd been on my back for weeks, I couldn't sit up without getting nauseous and passing out. So just starting at a twenty-degree tilt in the chair that first day was a challenge.

But Joanne knew what she was doing. She'd put me back down, let me rest a little bit, then get right back at it, pushing it another couple of degrees up. Then back down again. And back up. Again and again. It was agony. But by the end of the first day, we'd actually doubled the angle we started at. We were up to forty degrees.

The following days, we began working with something called a powder board, which is just that—a wooden board sprinkled with powder to reduce friction as something is rubbed across it. That something was my forearm. We'd put it on this board and I'd try to simply push it back and forth. There was a time when I could bench-press 430 pounds. And I could match anyone on squats—I could routinely squat 800. On the leg sled, I could lift 1,200 pounds—over half a ton. And now it was all I could do to push a skateboard a couple of inches.

From the day I arrived, Joanne was a bear about independence. I could hardly control my hand, so Joanne slid something called a "universal cuff" over my fingers—an elastic cuff with a leather pocket attached to the palm. She slid a fork or a spoon or a toothbrush into that pocket and then, using my bicep and wrist, I could lift food to my mouth or brush my teeth. It took me hours to do a task that took seconds before I was hurt. But *I* was doing it, and that was crucial.

*   *   *

That Sunday, my first weekend at Mount Sinai, Jeff came up and watched the game with me. It had been only a week since we'd played Buffalo, but it seemed like a year. That Bills game had been a passage for me, a farewell of sorts. Leaving Lenox Hill was, in a way, leaving what I had been before. Watching us play the Colts that afternoon made me realize what was happening. Those were still my teammates out there. They still loved me. They all came out to midfield before the kickoff, along with the Colts, and Marvin led them and the crowd at Indianapolis in a "Get Well" cheer for me. I was really moved by that. And I hated to see the guys lose that afternoon, especially to the Colts.

But I wasn't as wrapped up in it as I'd been the week before. I was in a different place now. I would

watch the rest of the games that season, but each time I did, I felt like I was seeing a ship slowly pull away from me, a ship I wasn't on anymore. Guys go through that feeling when they retire or when they're cut.

But it was different for me. I had just been getting started. I was still young. I wasn't even near the prime of my career when, in an instant, that tie was severed. I didn't get cut. I didn't get traded. I left not on my terms, not on the team's terms, but on God's terms.

I would always be a Jet. I knew that, and that feeling would always be precious to me. But I was something else now as well. I was paralyzed. I was in rehab. I was struggling every waking hour to take back my body. That was the entire focus of my life now. That, and my love for my wife and daughter, and my faith in the Lord. Those were the things that would see me through this. And I had no doubt I was going to get through it.

14

"You Will Walk Again"

Now it was coming on Christmas, and each day it seemed God was blessing me with another gift. So many things I was working on with Joanne and Lawrence were improving at a pace they said they'd never seen before. Every morning Joanne would rush in to see what new development I had to show her, usually a new muscle I could flex. I'd say, "Test it! Test it! Make sure it's real." She'd test it to see whether this was just tone kicking in or something I could really control. She'd have me twitch on command, and if I could, she'd shout "YES!" and do a little dance.

I wasn't sure how I'd feel if I got back my legs but not my hands. For the time being, I'd lost my hands, and it didn't look like they were coming back. This was one more thing I prayed about. I talked to the Lord about this, about handling the fact that I might not ever have the use of my hands again. I was intent on putting every ounce of effort and determination into getting them back, just as I was straining day in and day out to take back my legs. But if it wasn't to be, I prayed to God for the strength and wisdom to face it with courage.

One afternoon, just before Christmas, Angela and her brother Chris were in my room. We had all been reading the Bible together and praying, and now I was lying back resting while they sat nearby, talking to each other. I had my eyes closed. I was dog-tired, as usual, after another session downstairs, and I started sinking down into the gravity of all this. Usually I could keep myself on top of things. My willpower and faith and positive thinking kept me balanced, as if I were perched on top of a big ball. Occasionally, though, one of those things would begin to slip, I'd begin losing my balance, and the ball would start to roll over me.

That's how I felt lying in bed that afternoon. I'd made a lot of progress, but I was still so far from doing anything close to walking. I couldn't even lift my leg. I could flex some of the muscles, but I couldn't make it move. And my hands were so limp.

I wondered if I was truly strong enough to handle all this. I wondered if I could take it.

And then a voice came to me, a voice as clear as any I'd ever heard. And it said, "Be strong, my son. You will walk again."

I was shocked. I started crying. Angela and Chris looked over and had no idea what was happening. Ange came over and held me, asked me what was wrong, and I told her. Then they began crying, too. No moment in my life, before or since, was as strong as that one, the three of us crying together from the bottom of our souls, weeping with joy and awe, knowing that the Lord was with us.

Two nights before Christmas, I found myself in a familiar position—holding my hands up to my face and praying for movement, praying for feeling, praying until I was so exhausted I fell asleep. Late that night I was awakened by a buzzing in my hands. I couldn't move anything, but this was a feeling I'd never had. I remember looking at the clock. It was 3:00 A.M.

The next morning I called my mother in Baton Rouge. Before I could tell her what had happened, she told me she'd awakened in the middle of the night and had prayed for me. I asked her what time that had been. She said about 2:00 A.M.—3:00 A.M. eastern time.

That day I worked hard on my right index finger. I could feel it moving, even though neither I nor anyone else could actually see it. What felt like a tremor was too microscopic to see. But on the following day, Christmas Eve, came an earthquake. The finger moved, and Joanne was there to see it. Like the toe, it was barely a wiggle, just the slightest movement, but Joanne was out of there in a flash to let Dr. Ragnarsson know.

The next day, as she was driving with her fiancé to a friend's house for Christmas dinner, Joanne heard a report on the radio that my finger had moved! She said that really freaked her out. She hadn't realized until that moment how many people were paying attention to what was happening with me. She had been just like I was, ignoring the outside world and focusing entirely on our days together.

*   *   *

The first week in January, Joanne began working on my hands with something called Functional Electrical Stimulation. It's just what it sounds like, a machine that creates contractions in the muscles by applying an electric current to a specific spot on the skin. The thing Joanne did with the FES that was different than normal was, rather than simply sticking the electrodes on my thumbs or fingers, turning the machine on and watching, she had me do resistance exercises with her while the machine was on. For example, she would attach the electrodes to my hand, and the stimulation from the machine—a soft buzzing feeling, not painful at all—would make the hand open. As it opened, Joanne would push back against it, making me work with the machine against her own hands. She'd do that with the fingers and the thumb. With the machine's help, and with Joanne's coaxing, I was beginning to open and close my right hand by the end of the first week of January. I knew it was only a matter of time—about two weeks—that the same would happen with the left.

Even better was getting into the pool for the first time. This was the end of the first week in January, and it turned into a more monumental day than any of us expected.

We went down just after lunch, Lawrence and his boss, Roberta Weiss, head of the physical therapy department, and Joanne, too. I wanted Joanne to be there. Some of the other staff were there as well, including Dr. Ragnarsson. I rolled my chair up to a mechanical lift, and they transferred me into a harness seat attached to the lift by a chain. The lift then slowly swung me out over the water. I felt like a piece of meat dangling on a hook, but the sensation of slipping into that water was wonderful.

The plan was for me to do nothing more than float that day, with Lawrence and Joanne holding me up as I sat and helping me push my arms against the water, another form of resistance exercise. The water itself wasn't very deep, maybe waist high if I was standing.

I wasn't supposed to stand. Certainly not that day. But something told me it was time to try. Joanne was there and Lawrence, too, and there were parallel bars in the water.

Lawrence and Joanne floated me between the bars. It all happened so fast I don't think any of us had time to fully realize what I was doing—until I'd done it. With Lawrence and Joanne propping me up, I gripped the bars as best I could. My upper body rose out of the water. My feet found the bottom. My legs locked into place.

And just like that ... I was standing.

I couldn't believe it. I was *not* supposed to be doing this. The weight of my body, even waist deep in the water, felt incredibly dense, as if I were made of metal and a powerful magnet was under my feet. You don't have any idea what gravity is really like until you're paralyzed. The muscles are so weak that they can't carry the weight like before. It feels as if you're full of cement.

My sense of balance was just as out of whack. I hadn't been up in this position since I'd gone down on the field. I felt wobbly, as if I were standing on a flagpole.

But what I felt most was awe. And I felt hope flaring so brightly now it was like stepping into the sun.

Until then, I had believed I was going to walk again. Now I *knew*.

A few days later, I was back in the pool. And again, I stood up between the bars. But this time I went a little further. I lifted my right leg, pushed it forward, and set it back down. Then I shifted my weight to that side, lifted my left, and pushed *it* forward.

Walking.

I was walking.

The very next morning, Joanne took me down to the gym and set me on the edge of the mat. "Okay," she said, "today you're getting up. Today you're gonna walk."

She told me to start rocking forward—"nose over toes" was the way she put it. When my weight shifted, I should take that momentum and keep going, using my upper body strength and my gluts to push myself up into a standing position.

I did what she said. I rocked forward, pushed off, and came up.

I was up.

"All right now. Let's go for it," Joanne said.

With my arms leaning on a cart, I moved my right foot. Then the left. Then the right again. You could have heard a pin drop. Everyone was staring at us.

Eight steps and I was spent. But I had done it. Less than two months after my accident, I was *walking*.

15

A Jet Forever

We'd reached a crossroads, and I knew it. And I knew another thing: It was time to move on to the next stage. It was time to go home.

We set the date for February 12, a Friday. That meant we had to have a press conference. We wanted to say good-bye to the city we had come to love so much, the city we had made our second home, that had taken us in for four years and had helped take care of us for the past two-and-a-half months.

There was a battalion of reporters waiting as I came into the room. I could tell by the looks on their faces that they did not expect to see me walk in.

But I did, using my arm crutches, with Lawrence and Angela walking behind me. I'd been on my feet for some time now, but that was in private, with my therapists and with my family. This was the first time the public had seen it, and they were visibly moved. Even the *New York Times*, which rarely goes overboard with emotion, used a dramatic image to describe the moment.

"The scene," wrote Timothy Smith, the *Times*' reporter, "held the wonderment of Neil Armstrong's walking on the moon."

Dr. Ragnarsson spoke first, telling the audience I'd made "a remarkable recovery." "He has regained strength in virtually every muscle that used to be paralyzed," he said. "I think this is truly spectacular.

"I only wish I knew what the specific ingredient in his recovery was," he continued. Then he glanced over at me and added that he knew I knew the answer to that one.

As for my chances of ultimate recovery, he said, "There are a lot of unknowns. I don't think anybody truly knows."

Then it was my turn. I'd prepared a four-page speech, which was harder to read than I could have possibly imagined. "I'm very glad to be here standing before you today," I began. "I'm glad to be standing anywhere today."

A few nervous chuckles ran through the room.

"Obviously," I said, glancing up, "that was written down." That brought a roar of real laughter.

Then I settled into my speech. Step by step, person by person, I went through each stage of the model system of care I had received, singling out and thanking the people who had helped bring me to this point. It took a long time to get through the list. I choked up as I came to each person. Each name brought back vivid memories of that person's part in my experience. It was like reliving the entire seventy-six-day journey with the people who shared it.

Finally, I thanked the people of New York for their thousands of get-well letters and prayers. Then with more fresh tears welling up inside me, I came to the end, to the definition of who I had been when I first came to this city and who I had become as I prepared to leave.

"Four years ago," I said, "I came to New York a young Christian man."

I paused to draw my breath and fight back the tears.

"Now I go home a young Christian man and a New York Jet."

I had to pause again.

"I'm very proud to say that I'm a New York Jet," with the tears finally fighting their way out, "and I will be one forever."

16

Home Again

Owasso.

It's a word the Osage Indians used for a railroad depot built in the 1890s by the white settlers at a spot in northeast Oklahoma. In the century since it was built, that original depot has grown into a town of about eleven thousand people. But the name is still the same.

Owasso. It means "The End." It also means "Turnaround." And it is where I came home to that February afternoon with Angela and Ashtin.

It had been three years almost to the day since Angela and I had first moved into our house, six miles outside of town. In those three years, this place had become as essential to us as the clothes we wore or the food we ate. We had come to love New York, but there was no comparing the six months a year that we lived there with the feeling we had each time we came home to Owasso, to our lake and the trees and that familiar Oklahoma sky.

I could stand and walk now with forearm crutches, but it took a lot of effort, and it was only for short distances. And I was exhausted when I was done. Still, I resolved to use the wheelchair as little as possible. I used it when I went into Tulsa for my daily therapy session. When I was home, though, I got around under my own strength as best I could.

It wasn't easy. The staircase to our second floor is fourteen steps high, but it looked to me like the World Trade Center. Still, I resolved to climb it the first day I was home, and I did. It took me ten minutes, but I made it. And that meant I could play with Ashtin in her bedroom.

I was out to find and stretch my limits from my first day back. That Sunday—Valentine's Day—Angela and her parents were in the den talking. They didn't notice me slip away. I picked up my truck keys and worked my way out to the garage and up into the driver's seat of my Bronco. As soon as I started the engine, Angela came bursting out the door.

"Where do you think you're going?" she asked.

"I'm going for a ride," I said. "See ya."

And I backed out. I knew I had enough control in my right leg and both arms not to be endangering myself or my neighbors. But my neighbors didn't know that. One of them, Celeste Alford, was working in her yard as I drove past. She looked up and nearly fell over. I stopped to say hi.

"I don't believe this," she said. "You're supposed to be paralyzed. What are you doing in that truck?"

"Out for a Sunday drive," I said. And I put it in gear.

Monday I began my rehab in Tulsa's St. John Medical Center. I quickly found out that the staff there intended to push me just as hard as Joanne and Lawrence had. I was there five days a week, three hours a day, perfecting my walk and building my strength.

In medical terms, I was now a *quadriperesic*, rather than a quadriplegic. This meant my limbs, once paralyzed, were now very weak but functional. I still didn't have normal feeling from my shoulders down, but I could feel a constant burning sensation in my hands and feet, in my lower back and in parts of my legs. That was my signal that the nerves were activating.

One evening, early in the summer, something opened up inside and it all rushed in, all the memories and all the sorrow. For months I'd been totally focused on simply getting my body back. Except for brief moments, which I'd quickly put aside, I hadn't been able to sit back and fully feel the fact that I'd never play football again.

As I sat there on the sofa that evening, I was swept by the realization that it was all over. I'd regained the ability to walk. But I would never get back on the football field again. And that crushed me.

I started to cry. And I kept on crying, harder and harder, from a very deep place.

After a while, Ange came up to see how I was doing. She saw me there on the sofa, came over and took me in her arms, and that's where we stayed for the next forty-five minutes, weeping from the bottom of our hearts.

That was the hardest I'd ever cried in my life. It was good to have done that. It's a stage everyone is supposed to go through before he can truly leave something behind. They say you have to let yourself feel the hurt. Then you can go about the business of moving on.

I could easily have been destroyed by what happened to me. But there is a verse in 2 Corinthians about weakness: "He said to me, 'My grace is sufficient for you, for my power is made perfect in weakness.'"

Only in my weakness was I able to lay my entire life at Christ's feet. He had to fight the battle for me, and he did. Every place where Satan attacked me turned into a blessing. I feared that my wife would leave me, but she is beside me now as never before, with a love that has been tested by fire. I feared I would never hold my daughter again; I hold her today and she holds me back. And she has a little sister now who will hold me the same way.

I feared I might be abandoned, forgotten; instead I have been embraced and honored more than I ever could have dreamed. I've continued to be uplifted by the dozens of letters that still arrive in the mail each week from people I've never met who want me to know how much they care. How can a man ever show his gratitude for so much love and support?

I feared I would never have my legs beneath me again; they are here now, and they will only get stronger. There could be no better answer to what Satan tried to do to me than to walk out onto that Giants Stadium turf for the Jets' opening day game.

I have taken that walk. I always knew I would. Even when the fear was strongest, I still believed from the bottom of my heart that someday I would walk back out onto that field. I didn't know when, but I knew I would.

And now I have.